CarniFood

CarniFood

30 OF YOUR FAVORITE FAIR FOODS YOU CAN MAKE AT HOME

RECIPES BY AMY ERICKSON

WILLOW CREEK PRESS

Published by Willow Creek Press, Inc.
P.O. Box 147, Minocqua, Wisconsin 54548

Printed in China

INTRODUCTION

Tacky decadence never tasted so good. Cotton candy, corn dogs and candy apples once reigned supreme on the midway, but nowadays, festival enthusiasts are craving side-show amusements on a stick or freaky fried monstrosities. These eye-popping delights meld the crossroads of savory and sweet with next-level flavor bombs, unnatural relationships with pickles and peanut butter and an unabashed love affair with Flamin' Hot Cheetos®. If the Grilled Cheese & Tomato Soup Egg Rolls don't get you, the Bacon Fried Pop Tarts® will.

CHAPTER № 1
SWEETS

POPCORN DOGS

SERVES 6–8

Do you like popcorn? Do you like corn dogs? How about both of them together? The crunch and nutty flavor that the popcorn adds to the corn dog is seriously special and a dessert like no other.

INGREDIENTS:
- 6–8 bun length hot dogs
- 4–6 cups of popped popcorn

THE BATTER:
- 1-8.5 oz. box of corn bread mix
- 1¼ cup all-purpose flour
- ¼ cup white granulated sugar
- 1 tablespoon baking powder
- dash of salt
- 1 egg beaten
- 1½ cup buttermilk or regular milk
- 1 tablespoon vegetable oil
- 1 tablespoon honey
- wooden skewers
- oil for frying

DIRECTIONS:
1) Set your popcorn aside and in a large bowl, combine the corn bread mix, sugar, baking powder and salt.

2) In a medium bowl combine the milk, egg and honey.

3) Pour the wet ingredients into the dry, and combine, it should be like a thick pancake batter. Evenly coat the hot dogs with the batter (save the remaining) and then coat them with the popcorn. Not all the popcorn will stick.

4) Place them onto a parchment lined sheet pan and into the freezer for at least one hour.

5) When your oil is fully heated to 350 degrees, take out the hotdogs from the freezer and dip each frozen hot dog into the remaining batter.

6) Put them directly into the oil, fry them for a few seconds, until they're evenly golden on all sides, then they are ready!

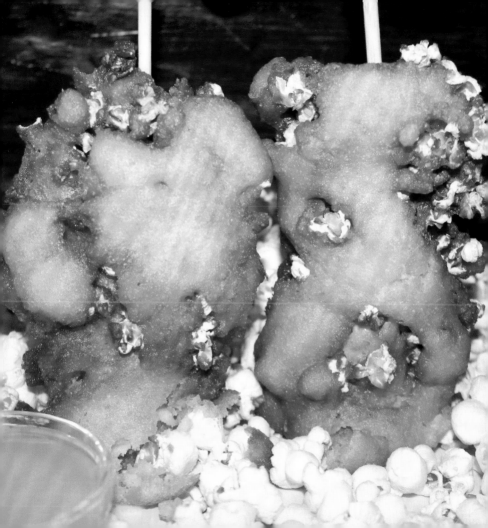

BACON FRIED POP TARTS®

That deep fried bacon has lovingly wrapped itself around that innocent classic breakfast food, the one and only Pop Tart®! An ooey-gooey Pop Tart® mixed with a smoky and crispy layer of bacon, drizzled with a sweet cascade of sprinkled frosting.

DIRECTIONS:

1) Wrap each Pop Tart® with 2 slices of bacon and secure with a toothpick.

2) Place them one at a time in the oil and fry until golden brown on both sides. Let them cool.

3) Drizzle each one with the frosting and a dash of sprinkles for that classic Pop Tart® experience.

INGREDIENTS:

- 1 lb. bacon thinly sliced.
- 3 packs of Pop Tarts®
- oil for frying
- optional: white frosting and sprinkles for garnish

FAIR FACTS

Carousels with wooden horses were first used to give horseback riding lessons to Turkish and Arabian cavalry members. The spinning attraction became especially popular in France, where 17th century riders tried to pierce a target while moving at high speeds. The power source? Actual horses!

APPLE PIE FUNNEL CAKE COOKIES

SERVES 4

These mini funnel cakes in cookie form will bring all of that state fair fun home to you. These are sweet, crispy and will be the life of your party.

INGREDIENTS:

- 3 eggs
- ¼ cup sugar
- 2 cups milk
- 1 tbsp. vanilla
- ½ cup pureed apple pie filling
- 3¼ cup flour
- ½ tsp. salt
- 2 tbsp. apple pie spice
- 2 tsp. baking powder
- oil for frying

TOPPING:
- ½ cup powdered sugar
- 1 tbsp. cinnamon

DIRECTIONS:

1) In a food processor or blender, chop up the apples until they're smooth.

2) Beat eggs, sugar and vanilla together and then add the milk slowly–beat. Add the smooth apple pie filling; continue to beat until ingredients are well blended.

3) Add the dry ingredients and beat until smooth and creamy.

4) Pour batter into a squeeze bottle or you can funnel the batter directly into the oil into cookie-like shapes.

5) Brown both sides, remove and pat oil dry on a paper towel.

6) In a small bowl, combine powdered sugar and cinnamon. Using a sifter, sprinkle cinnamon sugar mixture over the funnel cake cookies.

PUDDING CUP S'MORE POPS

Each icy cold pop is creamy and rich thanks to the pudding, and all of them have a magical marshmallow center that everyone seems to love almost too much!

DIRECTIONS:

1) Place a marshmallow on the end of a stick, open the pudding cups, and stick the marshmallow down into the pudding.

2) Sprinkle the tops with some graham cracker crumbs.

3) Put them in the freezer for a minimum of 2 hours.

4) Run the cup under warm water to loosen it up when ready to enjoy.

INGREDIENTS:

- chocolate or vanilla pudding cups
- marshmallows-one per pop
- graham cracker crumbs
- sticks

FAIR FACTS

Before she was Queen Bey, Destiny's Child played at state fairs in 1998 and 2001. That's right: even Beyoncé has hit the state fair circuit.

WAFFLE CRUSTED MAPLE BACON CREAM PIE

SERVES 6-8

The custardy, maple syrup soaked Belgian waffles become super toasty and are the perfect flavor-chamber for a rich, creamy, and decadent maple cream pie that's studded with maple bacon.

INGREDIENTS:

THE CRUST:
- 6 Belgian waffles
- 3 eggs
- ½ cup maple syrup
- 1-8" springform pan

THE MAPLE CREAM PIE:
- 1-15 oz. box of instant vanilla pudding
- 4 cups of Cool Whip
- ½ cup maple syrup
- ½ lb. of crispy and crumbled bacon

DIRECTIONS:

1) Prepare the crust. In a large bowl, combine the 3 eggs and the ½ cup maple syrup. Quickly soak both sides of each waffle in the egg mixture.

3) Cut the waffles into sections that will best fit the pan. Cover the entire surface of the pan.

4) Bake the crust at 350 degrees for approx. 15 minutes, or until the crust is golden. Let the crust cool completely and make the maple cream pie.

5) In a large bowl, mix up the instant pudding according to the box instructions. Fold in the ½ cup of maple syrup.

6) Fold in the Cool Whip, you can leave some lumps if you'd like, they'll be yummy, cold pockets of sweetness.

7) Pour mixture into the cooled waffle crust, making sure not to fill it above the lowest point of the crust.

8) Place in the freezer for at least 2 hours to firm up. Drizzle maple syrup over the waffles.

DEEP FRIED MAPLE BUTTER BALLS

SERVES 4

These balls are light, flavorful and fun, but it's the maple drizzle that really makes them amazing. It's so simple! They're moist, tender and filled with buttery goodness that literally melts in your mouth.

DIRECTIONS:

1) In a large bowl, combine the batter ingredients and mix well to combine, it will be a thick, dough-like consistency.

2) In a medium bowl, combine the filling ingredients, stir until smooth, and set aside.

3) Fry up approx. 1 tbsp. of the dough at a time until they are golden.

4) Let cool. Fill balls with a squirt of the buttery brown sugar filling.

INGREDIENTS:

THE BUTTER-
BALL BATTER:
- 2 cups all-purpose flour
- 12 tbsp. butter-melted.. (1½ sticks)
- 2 tbsp. granulated sugar
- 4½ tsp. baking powder
- 1 egg
- oil for frying.

THE FILLING:
(OPTIONAL)
- 1 tbsp. butter melted
- ¼ cup maple syrup
- ½ cup brown sugar
- 1 tsp. cinnamon
- optional: top with more maple syrup

CINNAMON ROLL CHIPS & DIP

SERVES 2-4

These are so unique, fun and are the perfect balance to all those savory chips and dip varieties that make it to every event or party. Why not have sweet options for chipping and dipping? This will become one of your go to snacks from now on!

INGREDIENTS:

- 1 roll of Pillsbury™ Cinnamon Rolls
- ½ cup cinnamon sugar
- flour for rolling them out
- oil for frying
- optional: extra frosting in case you need more "dip"

DIRECTIONS:

1) Roll out each cinnamon roll until thin and cut into four equal pieces.

2) Fry in the hot oil in small batches until golden brown.

3) Sprinkle generously with the cinnamon Sugar on both sides.

4) Serve chips with the icing for dipping.

CHICKEN & WAFFLE FUDGE

This fudge is not only surprisingly delicious, whimsical and fun, but it's also a super easy, and such a unique way to jazz up that classic chicken & waffle combo. The flavors really aren't any different than you'd find on your dinner plate, as the sweet, and savory are in complete harmony here.

DIRECTIONS:

1) In a large bowl, combine the frosting and the white chips, microwave for a few seconds at a time, stirring in between, until melted.

2) Stir in the brown sugar, cinnamon/sugar, pecans and extract.

3) Fold in chicken and stir until it is coated with fudge.

4) Add the fudge into your pan, and evenly smooth out the top, making sure that the chicken is evenly dispersed throughout. Put in the fridge for 15 minutes.

5) Take out and drizzle the top with some maple syrup. Place in fridge for 15 more minutes.

6) Cut into traditional fudge-like squares and serve!

INGREDIENTS:

- 2 cups of popcorn chicken (I got mine from the grocery store deli counter)
- 1-16 oz. container of white frosting, I used cream cheese flavor.
- 1-20 oz. bag of white chips
- ½ cup pecan chips
- 2 tbsp. cinnamon/sugar
- 1 tbsp. brown sugar
- 1 tsp. maple extract
- syrup for drizzling
- a square pan

GLAZED DOUGHNUT SNICKERS® WAFFLES

SERVES APPROX. 4-6

Nothing compares, or even comes close, to what the simple combination of sticky doughnuts and chewy Snickers® become when waffle-ized. They're undeniably, indescribably delicious, as the toasty and gooey waffle literally becomes one with the sweet, nutty Snickers®!

INGREDIENTS:

- waffle iron
- non-stick spray
- glazed doughnuts
- mini Snickers® bars

DIRECTIONS:

1) Slice the doughnuts equally in half, and place a few mini Snickers® bars onto the bottom half and place the other half of the doughnut on top like a sandwich.

2) Place it into the greased waffle iron, slowly closing it all the way.

3) Serve with ice cream, if desired!

FAIR FACTS

The Ferris wheel was invented by George W. Ferris for the 1893 World's Fair, which was held in Chicago to commemorate the 400th anniversary of Columbus's landing in America.

DEEP FRIED TEQUILA SHOTS

I really don't know how to describe these one of a kind treats, other than maybe try to envision a sweet and subtle tequila flavor all suspended inside a soaked until moist, melt in your mouth bite of sweet cake that tastes like funnel cake. That's what these are like!

DIRECTIONS:

1) Cube up the angel food cake into small squares.

2) Dip them quickly into the tequila.

3) Fry them up until they are golden on all sides.

4) Let them cool on some paper towel. Then make up your shot glasses if you'd like.

5) Dust with powdered sugar and enjoy!

INGREDIENTS:

- sponge cake/angel food cake (can be store bought)
- tequila
- oil for frying
- powdered sugar

PEANUT BUTTER FRIES

SERVES 4-6

Warm peanut butter fills each light-as-air, crispy, flaky, layer of these succulent sticks of joy. I'm not kidding, if you like peanut butter, if you like toasty, roasty and crispity-crunchity, these are for you!

INGREDIENTS:

- large egg roll/wonton wrappers: one per fry
- peanut butter: 1 tbsp. per fry
- powdered sugar for sprinkling
- jelly for dipping
- oil for frying

DIRECTIONS:

1) Spread the peanut butter evenly onto the wrapper and roll it up nice and tight.

2) Place them into the freezer for at least 1 hour, this gives the dough time to crisp up in the oil without losing any melty peanut butter.

3) Get them all lined up and put them in the hot (350 degree) oil. Fry them one at time; just until they're golden, this happens fast.

4) Top the fries with some powdered sugar for flavor and for pretty. Serving them in cups with some jelly at the bottom is super fun, and tasty too.

JELLY DOUGHNUT MONTE CRISTO

SERVES 4-6

When you eat this concoction you literally sink down, surrendering into that tender, sweet, jelly filled doughnut and when you get to that warm, cheesy, monte cristo meaty goodness, you'll think you died and went to sandwich heaven, and then you reach the OTHER jelly doughnut on the bottom. This is breakfast mixed with lunch mixed with love!

DIRECTIONS:

1) Simply layer your sandwich fillings on a plate and put them in the microwave until melted.

2) Place in between the two jelly doughnuts and make a sandwich.

3) Dig in. It's that simple!

INGREDIENTS:

- jelly doughnuts, 2 per Monte Cristo
- deli cheese (any variety)
- deli meat (any variety)

FAIR FACTS

Everything really is bigger in Texas—including the state fair. The State Fair of Texas has 3.5 million annual visitors, the highest attendance of any state fair in the United States.

DEEP FRIED BREAD PUDDING

SERVES 8–10

If you love bread pudding, if you love fried snacks, this is the tasty treat for you. Each custardy coated, crunchy~crispy, Kahlua-dipped bite will make you want more and more. This is a short and sweet recipe that you will make after dinner time and time again!

INGREDIENTS:

- 1 can of flaky layers biscuits
- 2 cups panko bread crumbs
- 1 cup milk
- ½ cup flour
- 1 egg
- 1 tsp. vanilla extract
- oil for frying

THE GLAZE:
- 1 cup of powdered sugar
- 2 tbsp. Kahlua, mix until thick.

DIRECTIONS:

1) Cut each biscuit into 4 equal sections, and roll them into a ball until you have 32 balls.

2) Mix together the milk, egg and vanilla, and dip each ball in the liquid.

3) Sprinkle on the bread crumbs.

4) Place in the oil and cook until they are golden on all sides.

5) For the glaze, mix up the powdered sugar and Kahlua until thick. Serve warm!

HOT CHEETOS® ICE CREAM

The balance of the heat & the sweet, the hot & the cool, the creamy & the crunchy, is nothing short of impeccable. These look crazy and wild and are fun, and are sure to please the fun at heart!

DIRECTIONS:

1) In a food processor, pulse the Cheetos® until they're crumbs.

2) Now add in the ice cream, and pulse until incorporated.

3) Dip the cones into the chocolate sauce and roll in Cheetos® crumbs.

4) Fill up the cones with the ice cream and enjoy.

INGREDIENTS:

- 2 cups crushed hot Cheetos®
- 2 cups vanilla ice cream
- ice cream cones: one per serving
- chocolate sauce
- ½ cup crushed hot Cheetos® for the cones

FAIR FACTS

The first annual fair in the American colonies was held in 1641 in New Amsterdam (now New York City) to showcase farm products of the local area.

STRAWBERRY SHORTCAKE TWINKIES®

Make a big batch of these on a hot summer day, toss them in the fridge and have a cool treat that everyone will love. Adding the all-American snack of twinkies, with fresh, red ripe strawberries, will make this a snack that everyone will be asking for more!

INGREDIENTS:

- Twinkies®
- 1 cup of melted white chocolate
- fresh strawberries: about 3 per twinkie
- skewers

DIRECTIONS:

1) Gently insert a stick into the bottom of a twinkie, and spoon some melted white chocolate over it.

2) Place sliced fresh strawberries onto the wet chocolate and place onto wax paper to set.

3) Cool in the fridge and serve on a hot day!

FAIR FACTS

What we call "Cotton Candy" was originally called "Fairy Floss" and was invented in 1897 by candy makers William Morris and John C. Wharton of Nashville, Tennessee. It was introduced at the St. Louis World's Fair in 1904.

CHAPTER № 2
SAVORY

FRITO PIE AVOCADO BOMBS

SERVES 2-4

Avocados have got to be one of my all-time favorite foods. Not only are they packed with tons of vitamins, they simply taste amazing, they're healthy and delicious. Each avocado bomb is coated in crushed Fritos®, filled with gooey & cheesy "ammo" and then topped with a hearty, generous scoop of chili.

DIRECTIONS:

1) Preheat oven to 350 degrees.

2) Crush half a bag of the corn chips into crumbs and place in a shallow bowl.

3) Lay out the remaining corn chips, plus some from the unopened bag if needed, evenly onto the sheet pan.

4) Evenly cut each avocado in half lengthwise, and remove the pit.

5) Coat each avocado half in the crushed corn chips and place them onto the sheet pan.

6) Place a 1″ cube of cheddar cheese into the center of each avocado and then add a huge dab of chili to the top.

7) Sprinkle cheese on top and bake for 15–20 minutes.

8) Top with garnishes and enjoy.

INGREDIENTS:

- 2 med avocados
- 2-9 oz. bags of corn chips
- 4-1″ cubes of sharp cheddar cheese
- 1 cup shredded cheddar cheese
- 1 cup of prepared chili

GARNISH:
- cilantro / jalapeños / mexican crema or sour cream

PIZZA HOT DOG BUNS

SERVES 4

This is the most dynamic culinary combo ever, as two of our favorite snacks has now become one. Mixing two American classics will be a crowd favorite for kids and adults alike. With two ingredients how can you not like this simple recipe?

INGREDIENTS:

- bun length hot dogs
- frozen pizza-defrosted
- grill or skillet
- tinfoil

DIRECTIONS:

1) Defrost the pizza, and cut it evenly in half.

2) Place the pizza, crust side down, onto the grill and lay the hot dog in the center.

3) Cover with a foil tent, until the pizza and the hot dogs are warm.

4) Gently fold the pizza in half, around the hot dog and serve!

FAIR FACTS

Sometimes it pays to check out the local talent when you go to the fair. Legend has it that Elvis sang in the youth talent show at the Mississippi-Alabama Fair and Dairy Show, and not only did he not win, he actually came in fifth place.

MASHED POTATO BACON BOMBS

SERVES 4

Do you ever have leftover mashed potatoes from dinner that you just can't stand to throw away? How about making a creamy, gooey, cheese-stuffed, deep fried mashed potato ball, coated in nutty bread crumbs and crispy, salty, bacon? Perfect bite size snacks!

DIRECTIONS:

1) In a large bowl, combine the mashed potatoes, egg, and salt and pepper until well blended.

2) Place a scoop of the mashed potatoes and gently form it around a cheddar chunk.

3) Add the bread crumbs in a shallow bowl and roll around the bombs.

4) Wrap the bomb with one slice of bacon and secure it with a toothpick or skewer.

5) Fry in about 2" of oil until they are golden brown.

6) Pat dry with a paper towel and serve with sour cream.

INGREDIENTS:

- 2 cups leftover and chilled mashed potatoes
- bacon: one slice per bomb
- 1 egg
- ½ cup dry bread crumbs
- cheddar cheese cut into 1″ chunks (one chunk per bomb)
- salt and pepper to taste
- skewers or toothpicks
- oil for frying
- optional for dipping: sour cream

SLOPPY JOENUTS

SERVES 4-6

Imagine for a moment, a doughnut. Just a simple, warm, tender, perfectly fried and fluffy orb of dough. Now imagine that doughnut stuffed at the seams with hearty, rich, decadent and classic, good old sloppy joe filling. This is a comfort food for the books!

INGREDIENTS:

- 1 container of Pillsbury™ Grands Biscuits
- 1 lb. lean ground beef
- 1 can of sloppy joe sauce
- 1 tbsp. toasted sesame seeds
- 2 tbsp. of melted butter
- oil for frying

DIRECTIONS:

1) Roll out each biscuit, so it's evenly round, and place a scoop of the sloppy joe filling into the center of the dough.

2) Wrap the dough around the filling, making sure to secure the dough together very well and set aside.

3) Fry them, one at a time, until they are evenly golden on each side.

4) Brush biscuits with melted butter and add a dash of sesame seeds.

5) Serve warm!

FLAMIN' HOT MEATOS

Each flamin' hot meatball is stuffed and coated with layers of crushed flamin' hot Cheetos®. Not to mention hot and melty mozzarella to cool the whole thing off, and a fiery fun edible hot Cheetos® toothpick.

DIRECTIONS:

1) Crush up the Puffs, and evenly separate the crumbs into two bowls and set aside.

2) In of the Puffs bowl, add the egg and the beef. Mix well.

3) Prepare the cheese into 1″ cubes.

4) Form the meat into small balls, and place a cube of mozzarella into the center surrounding the cheese with meat.

5) Place them on a lined sheet pan, and bake at 350 degrees for approx. 20–25 minutes until fully cooked.

6) Place the balls into the reserved PUFF crumbs, and generously coat them.

7) Insert a Cheetos® Crunchy Flamin' Hot "toothpick" into each ball for hand-to-mouth ease.

INGREDIENTS:

- 1-8oz. bag of Cheetos® Flamin' Hot Puffs divided in half
- 1 lb. lean ground beef
- 1 egg
- mozzarella cheese, cut into 1″ cubes
- optional: Cheetos® Crunchy Flamin' Hot for the "toothpicks"

FRIED PICKLE STUFFED ONION RINGS

SERVES 4

Sometimes things are just better together! It's almost like that hole in the center of the onion ring was made for a sassy slice of pickle. Top it all off with a crunchy coating of pretzels, and now the good times can begin!

INGREDIENTS:

- 2 medium onions
- pickle slices
- 2 cups crushed pretzels
- 1½ cups flour
- 1 cup panko bread crumbs
- 2 eggs
- 1 splash of milk or cream
- 1 tbsp. baking powder
- 1 tsp. paprika
- oil for frying

DIRECTIONS:

1) Crush up the pretzels and stir in the bread crumbs until well blended.

2) Set up 3 bowls: one with eggs and splash of milk. Second with flour with some paprika and third with pretzel crumbs mixture.

3) Slice up the onions into ⅛" rings.

4) Place one pickle slice into the center of the onion ring, and secure with a toothpick.

5) Freeze them for about 15 minutes.

6) Remove from freezer and coat each onion ring in flower, then dredge in the egg, followed by the pretzel mixture.

7) Fry until golden brown and enjoy.

SPICY CHURRO ELOTES

Elotes with churros, it's real, and it's spectacular! Sweet/spicy spectacular to be exact. Something about the cinnamon crunch over that spicy and creamy sour cream just works. Mixing these Mexican flavors is creative and a recipe you will want to try again and again.

DIRECTIONS:

1) Roast the corn on stove top grill or outdoor grill.

2) Mix the sour cream with the hot sauce, set aside.

3) Mix the honey with the chili powder and cayenne, set aside.

4) Let the corn cool and spread on the spicy sour cream.

5) Roll the corn in the crushed Cinnamon Toast Crunch.

6) Drizzle with the honey mixture and serve warm.

INGREDIENTS:

- 8 corn on the cob
- 3 cups of Cinnamon Toast Crunch cereal-crushed
- ½ cup sour cream
- 2–4 tbsp. hot sauce
- ½ cup honey
- 2 tbsp. chili powder
- dash of cayenne

GRILLED CHEESE & TOMATO SOUP EGG ROLLS

SERVES 4

Everyone loves the comfort food of grilled cheese and tomato soup, but how about in one finger food roll up? Perfect for kids play dates, football games or game night, these comfort foods mashed together will be sure to please all ages.

INGREDIENTS:

- 12 egg roll wrappers
- 12 cheese sticks
- 1 can of tomato paste
- oil for frying
- optional for dipping: 2 tbsp. butter, melted with a dash of parmesan cheese

DIRECTIONS:

1) Lay out a wrapper, and evenly smear 1 tbsp. or so of the tomato paste and lay one cheese stick diagonally across the wrapper.

2) Roll it up and secure with water.

3) Fry them until golden.

FAIR FACTS

You might think of cheese when you think of Wisconsin, but the most popular food at the Wisconsin State Fair is hands down the cream puffs. Over 350,000 of them are sold every year.

POUTINE POPPERS

Poutine is an incredible pile of fries, cheese and gravy that could easily shame even the most daring of snackers, if not by the mess they make, definitely by the sheer volume of the stuff that can be consumed in one sitting. Each crispy and tender poutine popper is bursting with melty cheese curds, coated in potatoes (chips), and then shamelessly plunged deeply into a glorious pool of warm brown gravy.

DIRECTIONS:

1) Freeze the cheese curds for at least 2 hours, or overnight if possible.

2) Add the eggs, flour, and crushed chips into separate shallow bowls.

3) Coat the cheese in the flour, followed by the egg, and dredge in the crushed chips.

4) Fry them until golden brown and serve with warm gravy.

INGREDIENTS:

- 2 cups of crushed potato chips
- 24-1" cubes of frozen cheese curds (or just cut up a block of regular cheese if you can't find curds)
- 1 cup flour
- 2 eggs
- oil for frying.
- brown gravy for dipping

CHEESY GARLIC BREAD HAND PIES

SERVES 4

These glorious little garlic bread hand pies are what a hungry man's dreams are made of. Each buttery, flaky, pie is stuffed with all things garlic bread. I'm talking butter, garlic, cheese, and did I mention CHEESE!?

INGREDIENTS:

- 2 containers of Pillsbury® seamless dough sheets (or regular crescents will work, just pinch those seams together)
- 2 tbsp. butter; melted
- 1 tsp. oregano
- 1 tsp. of chopped garlic
- 8 oz. of soft mozzarella sliced
- oil for frying
- 3" round cutter

DIRECTIONS:

1) Mix the chopped garlic with the melted butter and oregano.

2) Lay out the dough sheets and brush the butter mixture onto one of the sheets.

3) Slice the mozzarella into approx. ½" slices and add a single layer of the sliced cheese.

4) Place the top dough sheet onto the cheese, and gently roll it with the rolling pin just to stick them together. Cut out your pies with the 3" round cutter.

5) Use a fork to pretty up those edges, and make sure they stay put.

6) Fry until they are golden brown.

DEEP FRIED PEANUT BUTTER & PICKLES

The sweet and savory, crispy, deep fried version of this mash-up is nothing short of yummy. Putting two comfort foods of peanut butter and pickles creates the best crunchy, gooey snack.

DIRECTIONS:

1) Group together 2 like-sized pickles and set them onto the paper towel and dry them off.

2) Smear the pickles with peanut butter and place the second pickle on top like a sandwich.

3) Place them in the freezer for one hour.

4) Wrap them inside a wonton wrapper and secure them with the egg wash.

5) Fry them until golden and serve warm.

INGREDIENTS:

- pickle chips
- 1 tsp. peanut butter per pickle
- wonton/egg roll wrappers
- 1 egg with a splash of water
- oil for frying

FRIED CHICKEN HOT DOG BUNS

SERVES 4

Who doesn't love crispy, tender, beer soaked, flavorful slab of fried chicken. The flavors and textures together are divine, and you'll never look at fried chicken or hot dog buns the same again!

INGREDIENTS:

- 4 hot dogs
- 1 lb. of thin sliced boneless/skinless chicken breasts
- 8 oz. beer or water

BATTER:

- 3 cups all-purpose flour
- 1½ tbsp. garlic salt
- 1 tbsp. ground black pepper
- 1 tbsp. paprika
- ½ tsp. poultry seasoning
- 1⅓ cups all-purpose flour
- 1 tsp. salt
- ¼ tsp. ground black pepper
- 2 egg yolks, beaten
- toothpicks
- oil for frying

DIRECTIONS:

1) In one medium bowl, mix together 3 cups of flour, garlic salt, 1 tablespoon black pepper, paprika and poultry seasoning.

2) In a separate bowl, stir together 1⅓ cups flour, salt, ¼ teaspoon pepper, egg yolks and beer. Think pancake batter consistency.

3) Between 2 sheets of parchment paper, gently pound out one of the chicken breasts until it's approx. ⅛" thick. Place one hot dog in the center of the chicken, and secure the chicken around the dog with toothpick.

4) Then dip in the dry mix. Shake off excess and dip in the wet mix, then dip in the dry mix once more.

5) One at a time, place the wrapped dogs into the hot oil until golden on all sides.

6) Let them cool and serve with your favorite hot dog toppings.

FUNNEL CAKE TACOS

The festive and fun, slightly spicy funnel cake provides the best flavor balance for that tasty, taco-flavored ground beef and smooth, cool avocado! A few jalapeño slices scattered around with a nice drizzle of sour cream and your mouth will be in for a ride better than any state fair can give you!

DIRECTIONS:

1) In a large bowl, mix up the pancake batter according to package instructions, add the chili powder.

2) Add the batter into the ziplock baggie and cut off small snip at the tip of the bag.

3) Squeeze the batter into the oil in a circular motion, creating a round funnel cake, let it cook about one minute or so and then gently flip it over to cook the other side. Take them out when they're golden.

4) Let them cool. Top each funnel cake with taco toppings and enjoy.

INGREDIENTS:

- 1 cup pancake batter
- a pinch of chili powder
- oil for frying
- a ziplock baggie to use as a "funnel"
- taco toppings: the more the merrier

BACON CARMEL APPLES

SERVES 6

The balance of flavors and textures are incredible and these babies will satisfy any and every craving you might have. Nothing like a crisp apple, with some sweet and chewy caramel lovingly wrapped all around it, snuggled together as one, by that smoky and salty bacon!

INGREDIENTS:

- 6 apples
- 1 lb. bacon, cooked
- 1 bag of caramels unwrapped
- candy apple sticks

DIRECTIONS:

1) Melt the caramels according to the package instructions.

2) Insert a stick into each apple, and gently dip them into the melted caramel, making sure to let the excess drip away.

3) Place them onto some wax paper for a couple of seconds to cool a bit and slightly set up.

4) Carefully form each slice of freshly made bacon around the caramel apples, pushing it carefully so it sticks.

5) Let them set and enjoy.

DEEP FRIED CORN ON THE COB

The light, crispity-crunchity, crust snuggles the corn in the most luscious and loving way, trapping in every single drop of moisture and flavor. Who doesn't love corn and foods that are deep fried? This is the perfect combination of both!

DIRECTIONS:

1) In a medium bowl, combine the flour with the Cajun salt and pepper, and baking powder.

2) Lightly dust each piece of corn with the flour and set side.

3) Now add ¼-½ cup of water to the flour and mix it up, you're looking for a pancake batter consistency. Brush the batter all over the ears of corn.

4) Place them one at a time in the oil to fry until golden brown.

5) Add butter and salt, or any other favorite corn on the cobb toppings.

INGREDIENTS:

- 3 fresh ears of corn, cut in half
- ½ cup flour
- 1 tbsp. baking powder
- 1 tbsp. of Cajun salt and pepper to taste
- oil for frying.
- optional: butter and salt for end toppings

ABOUT THE AUTHOR

Oh, bite it!

That's what I say to anyone who refuses to taste one of my recipes… I'm always chasing someone around with a fork and telling them to open up! After an entire year of posting crazy culinary concoctions on social media, my family and friends "kindly recommended" that while they enjoyed the constant influx of sinful goodies, it might be time to try my hand at a food blog instead.

Thanks to that gentle push and scores of people seeking a food porn sugar rush, "Oh, Bite It" became the dream job I never knew I wanted. My recipe collection took on a life of its own, as I began to work as an influencer with brands like AOL, Pillsbury, Coca Cola, Swanson's, Walmart, Bravo's Top Chef, Whole Foods, just to name a few.

As a self-trained cook, I take a light-hearted approach to cooking and creating. I fear no recipe fail, love a fool-proof, time-saving shortcut and believe that ingredients don't have to be expensive to be delicious. I hope you enjoy this collection of ooey gooey treats and always remember, a full sink is the sign of a great day.